NEW YORK
JETS

PAT RYAN

CREATIVE EDUCATION INC.

Published by Creative Education, Inc.
123 S. Broad Street, Mankato, Minnesota 56001

Designed by Rita Marshall

Cover illustration by Lance Hidy Associates

Photos by Allsport, Wide World Photos, Campion
Photography, Sportschrome, Spectra-Action, Focus On
Sports and Duomo

Library of Congress Cataloging-in-Publication Data

Ryan, Pat.
　New York Jets/Pat Ryan.
　p.　cm.
　ISBN 0-88682-378-1
　1. New York Jets (Football team)—History.　I. Title.
GV956.N37R93　1990
796.332′64′097471—dc20　　　　　　　　90-41524
　　　　　　　　　　　　　　　　　　　　　　　CIP

Monday through Friday millions of commuters arrive in Manhattan. Over the bridges and through the tunnels the men and women journey to the island where they work all day. Eight hours later they make their way home to New Jersey, Connecticut, and the boroughs of New York City.

The Tri-State area of New York, New Jersey, and Connecticut is a megalopolis of over fifteen million people. Before 1959, this huge population had only one football team to cheer for, the New York Giants of the National Football League.

When the American Football League was born, the

A durable back from the sixties, George Nock.

1 9 6 0

League Opener: Under rainy conditions the Titans defeated Buffalo 27-3 in their first AFL game.

founders of the league wanted a team for the New York area. The new league was made up of eight teams in two divisions. The Western Division teams were the Oakland Raiders, Los Angeles Chargers, Dallas Texans, and Denver Broncos. The Eastern Division consisted of the Buffalo Bills, Boston Patriots, Houston Oilers and New York Titans.

Because "titan" is another word for giant, the new league obviously was trying to copy the established NFL. The new team in New York would not really grow up until it found a name for itself. How the Titans became the Jets is a story about a team finding its own identity.

THE EARLY YEARS

The early years of the franchise were stormy times. Today, many sports experts are surprised that the organization was able to rise out of the ashes to become Super Bowl champions. Considering their beginnings it's easy to understand why. The Titans began by playing to empty seats. The New York spectators weren't coming to the box office, and the franchise was in trouble. For example, in 1962 the Titans drew only 36,161 fans for the whole season. Soon it became a tradition for thousands of youngsters to be let in free just to fill the empty seats, but toward the end of the season even that failed to attract the kids.

Despite the problems, the Titans had players who were willing to play each week simply because they loved the game. The Titans became a team for the unwanted. One of the most talented athletes on the team of forgotten players was Don Maynard, a great receiver who played his college

Another Jet who loved the game, defensive end Marty Lyons.

Despite the talents of colorful Don Maynard, the team could only manage a 5-9 record.

ball at Texas Western. Maynard, a free agent from the Canadian Football League, was the first player to sign a contract with the Titans. He joined a group of NFL castoffs, free agents, and a few draft picks under coach Sammy Baugh.

The new league fit Maynard's style; he was a nonconformist. At one point management ordered everyone to wear ties, so Maynard defiantly knotted a necktie over his dirty T-shirt. Maynard would outlast the team's first owners and go on to set several team records, including most yards (1,434) and most touchdown receptions (88) in his twelve years with the team. "The key to our offense," said Weeb Ewbank, who succeeded Baugh as coach, "was the knowledge that the opposing teams would double-team Maynard. While they were watching him, we hit the other receivers."

Yet despite the talents of Maynard, the Titans struggled in the new league. In their first three seasons, New York failed to post a winning record. On the field, the team was losing. In the stands, the seats were empty. In the front office the team was going broke. Something had to change.

The New York team has had a history full of mavericks, and it comes as no surprise that the man who led them into the modern football era was a risk-taker. Sonny Werblin, former television executive, arrived just in time to save the franchise. Werblin was a show business man, and he saw pro football as a growing sport. He was convinced New York could support two teams, and he was determined to change the image of the Titans.

Werblin's purchase of the bankrupt team was announced to the press on March 15, 1963, two days before St. Patrick's Day, Werblin's fifty-third birthday. Werblin wasted no time in making changes to his team. He began by changing the colors of the club from blue and gold to kelly green and white. Along with the new colors Werblin needed a new name, a name that would launch the team into a new era. So the Titans became the New York Jets and from that moment on the team soared.

The Jets posted the first shutout in team history with a 17-0 victory over Kansas City.

Werblin's next move was to bring in a coach who was an established winner. Weeb Ewbank, who had coached the Baltimore Colts to the NFL championship, would be the man. Ewbank was known for his ability to work with rookies, so he was a natural choice for a team that was starting over like the Jets.

Ewbank cautiously built the foundation for his new team one brick at a time. He first concentrated on the defense, acquiring players like 300-pound defensive tackle Sherman Plunkett and linebacker Gerry Philbin. On offense, Ewbank had Maynard and other fine receivers in place, but he needed someone to get them the ball.

Despite all the changes the Jets finished in last place with a 5-8-1 record in 1963. But Ewbank had convinced New Yorkers that the Jets were headed for great things. The fans for the first time flocked to the Polo Grounds, nearly tripling the previous attendance levels.

Ewbank added one more brick to his foundation in 1964 when he drafted Matt Snell out of Ohio State. Snell had

In the eighties, Freeman McNeil continued a tradition of fine Jet backs.
(pages 10–11)

*Super Snell! AFL
rookie of the year
Matt Snell gained
948 yards and
caught 56 passes.*

been a standout in college and Ohio State coach Woody Hayes urged Ewbank to give Snell a chance to carry the ball often in the pros. Ewbank followed Hayes's advice, and Snell had a record rookie year.

The Jets fans had something to cheer about at last. The newly acquired defensive lineman Wahoo McDaniel was chasing quarterbacks, and Snell was crashing through the line. The fans poured into the Jet's new home, Shea Stadium. By the end of the season, more than 300,000 fans had attended seven home games.

With plenty of money in the bank, Werblin gave Ewbank the order, "Go get him, coach!" Werblin was referring to the number-one pick in the 1965 college draft: the highly touted Joe Namath, an all-American quarterback from the University of Alabama. Ewbank didn't hesitate; he simply beat the NFL to the punch, signing Namath the day after he completed his college career in the Orange Bowl. "Name your price and it's yours," said Ewbank. In a contract that would shock the sports world, Namath agreed to sign for $427,000! Overnight, he became the highest-paid athlete in any sport. For the first time the AFL had outbid the NFL, and Namath would be the blue-chip player who would bring the AFL and the Jets into the big leagues.

Joe Willie Namath's rise to fame from a small town in Pennsylvania reads like a fairy tale. People who saw him play in high school knew early on he had greatness within him. Like many great football stars, Namath was an all-around athlete. Bubba Church, a former pitcher with the Philadelphia Phillies and one of Namath's friends, said of him, "In basketball he'd play against guys 6-feet-8 and he'd block—yes, block—their shots. He could dunk a ball two-handed with his back to the basket." "You name it," said friend Fred Klages, "Basketball, football, baseball, pool. There was nothing Joe Namath couldn't do, and do better than anybody else. He could walk into a pool hall and run a rack, then walk down the block to the gym and shoot twenty straight foul shots."

Originally, the Jets wanted to bring Namath along slowly, but when they went down to defeat in their first two games in 1965 the coaches decided to give him a chance. The rookie was asked to start the third game, against Buffalo. The Jets lost, but Namath showed he could move the team against the best defense in the league.

Namath had made his mark on the league. The Raiders' Al Davis called him "the kind of player who alters defensive game plans." Former Oakland Raider coach John Madden was particularly impressed with Namath's quick release. He later said, "Joe Namath had it. Terry Bradshaw had it. Roger Staubach had it. Kenny Stabler had it. Joe Montana and Dan Marino, have it now. But of all those great quarterbacks, I always thought Joe Namath had the quickest release.

"Broadway Joe," as Namath was known, was living up to everyone's expectations. The only question remaining was whether or not Namath's knees could hold up; they had been on ice throughout his college career. His fans wondered from season to season: How long could Joe gut it out?

The 1966 season would find Namath once again on his game, throwing bombs to the newly acquired George Sauer, Jr. and the veteran Don Maynard. The Jets ended the season by defeating the mighty Patriots to give Ewbank

1 9 6 5

More good things to follow—Joe Namath throws for two touchdowns in his first NFL start.

13

1 9 6 7

Winners! The Jets recorded their first winning season in the club's eight-year history.

his first break-even season (6-6-1) with the team. The Jets appeared to be on the verge of great things, but Namath was again wobbly. He would have to undergo surgery on one of his knees.

The football world was watching as Namath took the field for training camp in 1967. "He has more mobility by far than at any time since I've seen him," Ewbank proclaimed. A week later, Namath dropped back to pass and pain shot through his other knee. He would once again have to play with an injury.

Namath's courageous play, along with the performance of the Jets' new threat, running back Emerson Boozer, led the team to it's best record ever. Only four years earlier the Jets had been the laughingstocks of the AFL. By opening day in 1968 the oddsmakers were now picking the kelly green and white to land a Super Bowl berth.

JOE WILLIE'S GUARANTEE

It has been said that one player doesn't make a championship team, and this was true of the 1968 Jets. Besides Namath, Ewbank had a solid backfield in place with the one-two punch of Emerson Boozer and Matt Snell. The defense was also strong. It was led by all-pro Johnny Sample in the secondary and Al Atkinson at linebacker.

All of the bricks were in place for Ewbank's foundation for a championship team. The Jets won the Eastern Division in 1968 with a record of eleven wins and three losses. They were only a game away from the Super Bowl. But the Western Division champion, the Oakland Raiders, were ready to end the Jets' miracle. In a game in which the lead see-sawed back and forth, the Jets finally came out on top

Like Don Maynard, Al Toon is a big play receiver.

Super squad! Don Maynard was one of eleven Jets to be named to the AFL's All-Star team.

when Namath rocketed a pass to Maynard, knocking him down in the end zone. But Maynard held on and the Jets won 27-23. The New York Jets were headed to Miami for Super Bowl III.

Many football historians think Super Bowl III was the most influential game in professional football history. It was more than just a game between two teams, it was also a war between two leagues. The press was alive with insults from each side. The AFL was called the "Mickey Mouse league" by some people in the NFL. One Baltimore reporter wrote, "Let's face it, the AFL is strictly second-class. It will never win a Super Bowl." In New York, Broadway Joe countered with, "Our team is better than any NFL team. We will win the Super Bowl. I guarantee it."

Super Bowl III was just a few hours away. The Baltimore Colts were eighteen-point favorites, and Colts' owner Carroll Rosenbloom was getting ready for the victory party. "I'll never forget Carroll telling me before the game about his party," Ewbank said years later. "I told him I appreciated the invitation, but I was hoping I'd have my own victory party to attend that evening." The stage was set for what would go down as one of the greatest football games in history.

Behind closed doors the underdog Jets were convinced they could beat the Colts. Ewbank had spotted weaknesses in the Colts' secondary, and he knew the Colts would key on Don Maynard. The plan was to make George Sauer the target for the day.

Finally the game began. The Colts got a real surprise when Namath handed the ball off to Matt Snell, and Snell burst through the line for big yardage. With their ground game established, the Jets ambushed the Colts and their

Mark Gastineau ('79–88) attempted to carry on the legacy of the '69 Jets.
(page 17)

Gastineau and teammates wrap up Walter Payton. (pages 18–19)   17

young coach Don Shula. Baltimore's secondary keyed on Maynard just as Ewbank had forecast. George Sauer was able to break away and catch eight passes for 133 yards. On the ground, Snell gained 121 yards on thirty carries as the Jets defeated the Colts 16-7.

In the Jets' locker room after the game, NFL Commissioner Pete Rozelle was greeted with the words, "Hey Pete, welcome to the AFL." The Jets had received support from all of the teams in the AFL, so they felt it was appropriate to honor all of the players in the league. "This ball," said Johnny Sample, "belongs to the whole AFL."

All around New York, Jets' fans were talking dynasty. Namath's arm would take them back to the Super Bowl, they all thought. Unfortunately, his knees wouldn't be able to stand up over the long haul. The Jets had soared high in a few short years, and just as rapidly they would return to earth. A series of nagging injuries to Snell and Boozer, as well as Namath's battered knees, quickly grounded the Jets.

Over the next few years Namath would continue to mount comebacks, but although he played heroically, the Jets could not climb back to the top. Over the next several years much of Jets' talented cast would call it quits. Coach Ewbank retired, as did Sauer, Snell, and Maynard. It was time for a new beginning in New York.

A NEW ERA

In 1976 Lou Holtz became the Jets' new coach, and began a youth movement by signing quarterback Richard Todd. Joe Namath would pass the torch to a fellow Alabaman. Broadway Joe packed up his white shoes and moved to L.A. to end his career with the Rams. He completed his eleven years with the Jets with over 27,000 yards passing and 170 touchdown passes. The Namath era had officially come to an end.

In 1977 a disenchanted Lou Holtz left the Jets, and the popular Walt Michaels was elevated to head coach. Coach Michaels started the season with a second-year quarterback, Todd, and fourteen rookies, including receiver Wesley Walker and defensive tackle Joe Klecko. Michaels had been a defensive coach, and his team of the future would win games with defense and a new attitude.

1 9 7 8

Wesley Walker was the NFL's leading wide receiver as he tallied nearly 1,200 yards.

The Jets were on their way back to respectability with an 8-8 record in 1977. A sudden-death loss to the Cleveland Browns kept the Jets from reaching the playoffs, but Michaels reached the winner's circle personally when he was voted NFL Coach of the Year. It was clear to New York fans that the Jets were just a few draft picks away from a shot at the title.

One of the Jets' talented draft selections over the next couple years was defensive end Mark Gastineau, who joined the team in 1979. Together with Joe Klecko, they began building the "New York Sack Exchange." Klecko was a down-home boy who loved fast cars and went about his business. His partner, Gastineau was a different kind of defensive lineman: a showman with speed. Gastineau changed the perception of what defensive linemen were supposed to be.

"Going up against Gastineau," said Marvin Powell, the Jets' all-pro tackle, "is like going up against the Indy 500. He accelerates with speed and finesse. He can shake and bake you and leave you standing there. He can do anything he wants."

21

New York Jets' running back Johnny Hector.

Gastineau made all-pro five times. His greatest notoriety, however, may have come with what was called the "Gastineau Rule." After he made a sack he would do a sack dance. "I've never choreographed it," laughed Gastineau. "It comes from total joy and excitement. When I make a quarterback sack, it's an emotional high. It's a feeling I can't explain. I'd like to let everybody feel that way." The owners of other NFL teams didn't see much joy from this dance. They soon passed a rule to outlaw Gastineau's dance but Gastineau didn't let that stop him from sacking the quarterback.

In 1981 Michaels added another element, an all-purpose back who went on to become the Jets' all-time leading rusher. Freeman McNeil started his rush to the record books at UCLA. McNeil was the number-one pick for the Jets in 1981, and he brought instant success. The Jets made it to the play-offs for the first time in thirteen years, with a season record of 10-5-1.

The Jets faced their upstate rivals the Buffalo Bills in the first round. Misplays, fumbles, and interceptions put the Bills up 24-0 early in the second quarter, but the Jets didn't lie down. They rallied behind their talented quarterback, Richard Todd. With eleven seconds remaining, Todd had a chance to win the game, but Buffalo safety Bill Simpson intercepted his pass and the Bills won 31-27.

Coach Michaels remarked, "If all of New York hasn't already fallen in love with this team, then they will in 1982." Indeed the Jets continued their winning ways the next season. In fact the Jets got into the second round of the playoffs before losing to Miami 14-0.

The 1980s continued with Michaels and the Jets playing a game of "maybe next year." Disappointed, Walt Michaels

1 9 8 1

Quarterbacks beware: Joe Klecko combined with Mark Gastineau for a total of 40½ sacks for the season.

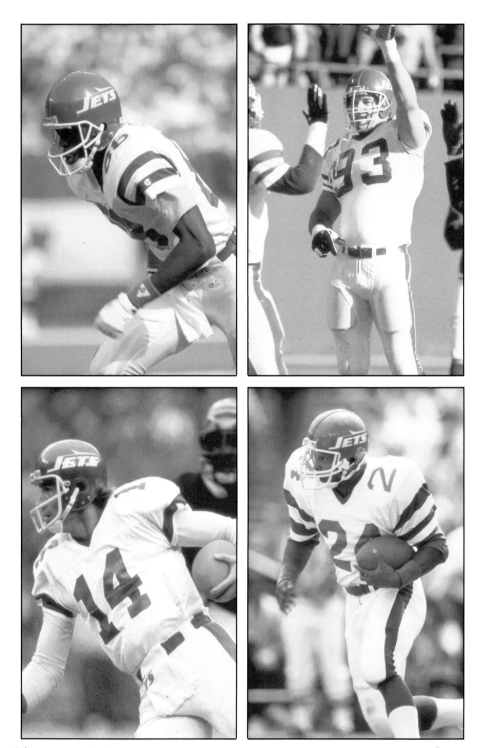

Clockwise: Al Toon, Marty Lyons, Freeman McNeil, Richard Todd.

resigned in 1983 and was hired to coach the New Jersey Generals in the United States Football League. Assistant coach Joe Walton was promoted to head coach. The Jets' front office also tried making a move to change the team's luck. It moved the team from Shea Stadium to Giants Stadium in New Jersey.

But great performances like Freeman McNeil's team record of 1,331 yards rushing in 1985, were all Jet fans had to cheer about through the remainder of the eighties. By the time the decade came to a close the Jets looked like the team that had come into the league in 1959. Joe Walton was given his walking papers at the end of the 1989 season as his record had fallen below five hundred. Walton's stay of seven years was the longest of any coach in the American Football Conference without having won a division title.

1 9 8 5

Offensive eruption! The Jets scored the most points in team history, trouncing Tampa Bay 62-28.

THE NINETIES BRING NEW HOPE

The nineties brought hope with the signing of new head coach Bruce Coslet. General manager Dick Steinberg said, "We needed a guy to change the environment." Coslet was the architect of the Cincinnati Bengals' high-tech, unnerving no-huddle offense. One of his former mentors, Bill Walsh, described Coslet's coaching as at "the cutting edge of the game."

Coslet, a one-time Bengal tight end who stands 6 feet 3 inches tall is a strict disciplinarian who will bring his formidable personality to the sidelines. "We're going to be a tough, aggressive, physical team," remarked Coslet, "and if you're not that, you won't play."

Coslet will need a strong offensive line to be successful. (pages 26–27)

Defensive back Erik McMillan was named to his second consecutive Pro Bowl.

Dick Steinberg is hoping that Coslet can create an offense and build a defense. After he was given the job, Coslet wasted no time; his first act as head coach was to hire former Minnesota secondary coach Pete Carroll as his defensive coordinator. Carroll likes tough, hard-working defensive backs, and he has one in free safety Erik McMillan.

Erik McMillan, who has only been in the league for a few years, has already made it to the Pro Bowl, and he plans to make it to several more. He played his college ball for the Missouri Tigers. McMillan made his presence felt there with a career record 203 solo tackles. He also tied an NCAA record as a senior by returning three interceptions for touchdowns.

McMillan's father Ernie was an All-Pro tackle with the St. Louis Cardinals, and today he is Erik's biggest fan. His father was scouting Erik when he was only nine months old. "Erik used to pick up these heavy fireplace pokers." said the elder McMillan. "He'd put one in each hand and walk around the room. That showed me he had decent hand coordination and good strength in his body." Erik McMillan grew up strong and quick. In the pros he put his strength together with a tough attitude. "I never had a doubt I could play at this level. I feel very confident," he said.

The young McMillan has become very unpopular with a few people in the league. Quarterbacks Dan Marino, Jim Kelly, and John Elway don't appreciate what McMillan does with their passes: he intercepts them or swats them out of the air.

Over one five-game span in 1989, McMillan had three touchdowns while the entire offense had only one. He will

Ken O'Brien was a key figure in the 1991 Jet attack.

McMillan and James Hasty (#40) gave New York a strong secondary.

Jets' kicker Pat Leahy.

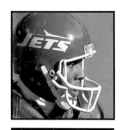

The Jets looked to wide receiver Al Toon to lead their offensive attack.

be the cornerstone of Coslets' defense in the next decade. "We want to achieve," said McMillan. "We want to get the fans and the team into it and let the other teams know we're going to war."

McMillan is not alone in his philosophy; his good friend James Hasty shares it. Hasty plays right cornerback, and he has showed no respect to the old-timers in the league. They are joined by another young hopeful, Jeff Lageman. Lageman, the 6-feet-5, 250-pound linebacker out of Virginia, plays with great intensity. The Jets believe he will get better, and hope his new defensive end position will help his sack numbers. Lageman, McMillan, and the rest of the Jet defenders are ready for the nineties.

On offense, Coslet must find out if veteran Ken O'Brien can get the ball to Al Toon. In 1988 Toon led the AFL in receptions with ninety-three for 1,067 yards. Toon, out of the University of Wisconsin, had caught at least three passes in over 50 consecutive games through 1989. He represents the deep threat the Jets so desperately need.

The Jets' future high draft picks and Coslet's ideas should make the team competitive again. "Coslet is a steal for the Jets," said Cincinnati quarterback Boomer Esiason "He knows more about how to dissect a defense than anyone I've ever seen. He wasn't only my teacher, but my eyes."

Coslet's eyes are now on the Jets' future. Because the Jets traditionally have been underdogs, they probably will be seen the same way in the nineties. But if their opponents take the Jets too lightly, they could be in for a shock. The next surprise team of the NFL may very well be the soaring Jets.